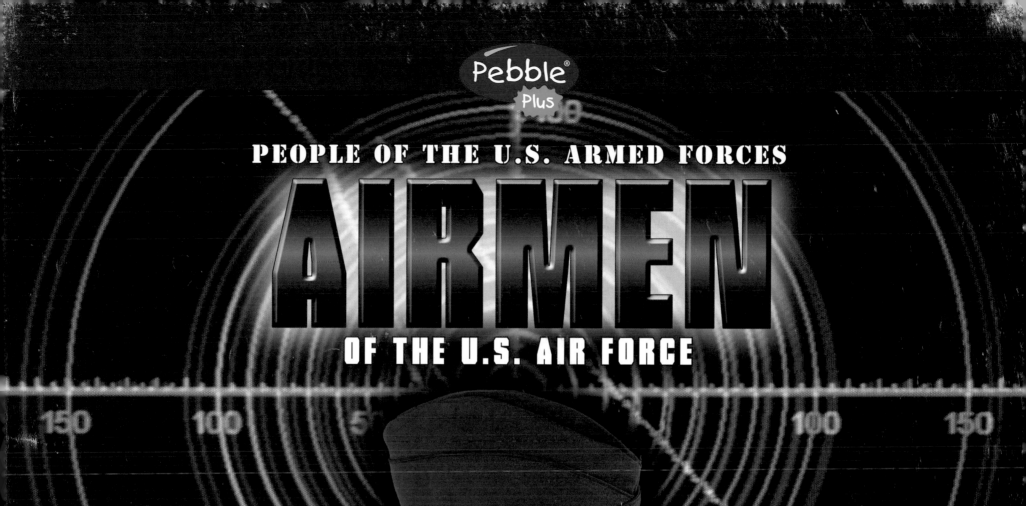

Pebble® Plus

PEOPLE OF THE U.S. ARMED FORCES

AIRMEN

OF THE U.S. AIR FORCE

by Lisa M. Bolt Simons

Consulting Editor: Gail Saunders-Smith, PhD

Consultant: Raymond L. Puffer, PhD
Historian, Ret., Edwards Air Force Base History Office

Capstone
press®

Mankato, Minnesota

Pebble Plus is published by Capstone Press,
151 Good Counsel Drive, P.O. Box 669, Mankato, Minnesota 56002.
www.capstonepress.com

1 2 3 4 5 6 14 13 12 11 10 09

Library of Congress Cataloging-in-Publication Data
Simons, Lisa M. B., 1969-
    Airmen of the U.S. Air Force / by Lisa M. Bolt Simons.
    p. cm. — (Pebble plus. People of the U.S. Armed Forces)
    Includes bibliographical references and index.
    Summary: "A brief introduction to an airman's life in the Air Force, including training, jobs, and life after
service" — Provided by publisher.
    ISBN-13: 978-1-4296-2249-3 (hbk.)
    ISBN-10: 1-4296-2249-0 (hbk.)
    1. United States. Air Force — Juvenile literature. I. Title.
UG633.S496 2008
358.4'1330973 — dc22   2008026968

Editorial Credits
Gillia Olson, editor; Renée T. Doyle, designer; Jo Miller, photo researcher

Photo Credits
Capstone Press/Gary Sundermeyer, 21; Karon Dubke, 1
DVIC/Sgt Olan A. Owens, 15
Getty Images Inc./Joe McNally, 9
Renée Doyle, 7
SuperStock, Inc./StockTrek, cover
U.S. Air Force photo, 17; by Master Sgt. Andy Dunaway, 5; by Master Sgt. Val Gempis, 11; by Randy Rubattino, 13;
    by Tech Sgt Howard Blair, 10; by Tech Sgt. Chance Babin, 19

Artistic Effects
iStockphoto/luoman (radar screen), cover, 1, 24
Shutterstock/Jamey Ekins (cockpit view), 22–23; Shutterstock/The Labor Shed (control panel), 2, 24

Note to Parents and Teachers

The People of the U.S. Armed Forces series supports national science standards related to
science, technology, and society. This book describes and illustrates airmen of the U.S. Air
Force. The images support early readers in understanding the text. The repetition of words and
phrases helps early readers learn new words. This book also introduces early readers to
subject-specific vocabulary words, which are defined in the Glossary section. Early readers
may need assistance to read some words and to use the Table of Contents, Glossary, Read
More, Internet Sites, and Index sections of the book.

Table of Contents

Joining the Air Force

Men and women join

the United States Air Force

to protect the country.

They defend the skies

and space.

Recruits go to basic training

in Texas for eight weeks.

They exercise and study.

They learn to march

and to shoot.

Job Training

After basic training,

recruits are called airmen.

Then, they train for their jobs.

Crew chiefs fix planes,

like the F-22 Raptor.

9

Some airmen become pilots.

They fly planes.

Pilots use the C-130 Hercules

to carry airmen and supplies.

Some airmen control radar.

They use radar to watch

the sky and space.

Living on Base

Most airmen live on bases.

Bases have homes, stores,

and hospitals for airmen

and their families.

Bases are in the United States
and around the world.
Airmen often move
to another base
every four years.

Serving the Country

Most airmen serve

for four or six years.

Career airmen stay

in the Air Force

for 20 years or more.

19

After serving, airmen leave

the Air Force to be civilians.

Some go to college.

Others use their skills

and training to find jobs.

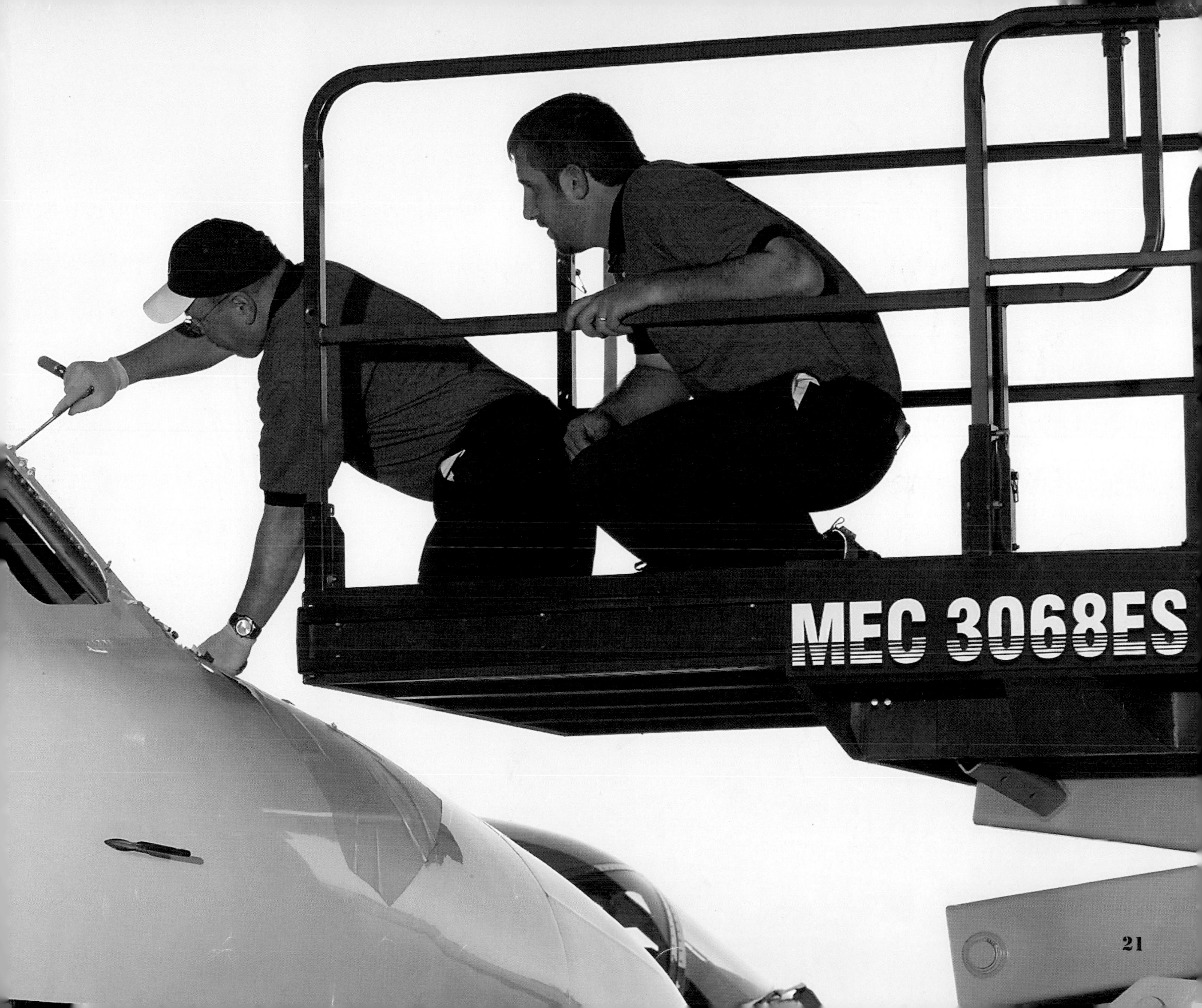
MEC 3068ES

Glossary

base — an area run by the military where people serving in the military live and military supplies are stored

basic training — the first training period for people who join the military

career — relating to the type of work a person does

civilian — a person who is not in the military

college — a school that students attend after high school

crew chief — a person who fixes airplanes and other machines in the Air Force

radar — equipment that uses radio waves to find and guide objects

recruit — a person who has just joined the military

Read More

Braulick, Carrie A. *U.S. Air Force Spy Planes.* Military Vehicles. Mankato, Minn.: Capstone Press, 2007.

Doeden, Matt. *The U.S. Air Force.* Military Branches. Mankato, Minn.: Capstone Press, 2009.

Hamilton, John. *Defending the Nation*: The Air Force. Edina, Minn.: Abdo, 2007.

Internet Sites

FactHound offers a safe, fun way to find educator-approved Internet sites related to this book.

Here's what you do:

1. Visit *www.facthound.com*
2. Choose your grade level.
3. Begin your search.

This book's ID number is 9781429622493.

FactHound will fetch the best sites for you!

Index

Word Count: 170
Grade: 1
Early-Intervention Level: 22

DATE DUE

HIGHSMITH 45230